CU00941253

# THE
# MANIFESTO
# OF
# *COMMON*
# *SENSE*
By

J.K. Adams

*This book is dedicated to my family:*
*My loving and very patient wife, Michelle and*
*my amazing kids.*

# Contents

Introduction

Who am I?

# Introduction

As we have just gone another general election, seeing the Etonian contenders for the throne of 'Prime Minister of Great Britain' battle it out, this has inspired me to create a manifesto, not full of political swipes and grovelling, but of common sense and hard truths.

BE WARNED!
This manifesto may contain policies that you don't like and may find offensive.

Please note: I really do not care.

As a very well-known comedian says "Being offended is a point of view, what offends you, may not offend me and vice versa." Just remember the saying 'Sticks and Stones' and you'll make it through!

So sit back and enjoy, what I hope is a good read and stirs the activist in you!

# Who am I?

I was born in Devon in the late 1980's. I am the youngest son in a family of four. My father was a royal marine, when I was born, my father left the marines and we moved to Bristol, which was a lot different back then, now it's a thriving, trendy city.

We lived in a no thrills three bed council house which my parents being born in the right era, were able to purchase from the government.

As a child I was very quiet, the benefit of which, is you pick up on adult conversations. I used to sit at the dining table at meal times listening to my father talking about politics. My father use to work for a trade union, so of course, is a devout Labour follower and for a short period, stood as a candidate for Labour in one general election. As this was during the decade of Conservative rule, he never got elected.

I attended school at the local state secondary, and learned everything except probably what I needed to.

As you can imagine, growing up my political influence was driven by my father. There was almost an expectation when I came of voting age to follow the family's political persuasion. Never being taught anything else, I followed suit.

As I grew up and had children of my own, my priorities changed, near the end of Blair's rule, I became disillusioned and started to question the family whip.

I started researching political terms, the history of the different parties, if I came across anything I didn't understand, I googled it.

Doing my own 'in the moment' research, and many wine fuelled political debates with my father, is how I built the understanding I have today, be it right or wrong.

My political persuasion changed from Labour (to my parent's dismay) and has changed a few times since, I am not what you would call a devout one party person. As those leaders changed and cabinet or shadow cabinet changed, the parties policies and principles changed, so I do not see how it is possible to be a one party person.

What I ended up seeing from each party, is broken promises, inaction, weakness and inefficiency.

Always instead of working for the overall picture of a better society and way of life, these parties are scoring cheap shots and having party in-fighting for political gain.

Now I am, heading towards middle aged, with a family gradually heading towards adulthood.

I decided to share my thoughts in the form of this book.

I see myself as an honest, hardworking, family man, from humble beginnings and like to merit myself as a bit of a problem solver.

But I'll let you decide......

# THE
# MANIFESTO

# EDUCATION

Educational reform has been required for a while now and the changes that have been made more recently do not seem to be from a stand point of increasing knowledge and opportunities.

This is what I would do to address that:

**Add the subject of 'Politics' to the state curriculum.**

**Pass legislation to teach only the basic principles of Sex Education in primary schools.**

**Create grants for local trades people to be contracted to colleges to create apprentice employment placements.**

**Adult Courses – Increase the variety of available Free Adult Learning Courses, to provide key skills, to fill key areas.**

**Implement 'National Service Weeks' to provide experience and exposure to civic services and the Armed forces.**

Immediately, I would add the subject of politics to our curriculum in state schools. I cannot believe we live in a democracy, but do not deem it necessary to educate our children about democracy. How can the average person make educated decisions without the knowledge to do this?

The fact that only private schools teach politics, along with the skill of debating, shows why the political system is dominated by 'private school' MPs, instead of proper representation of all wealth categories.

By doing this, it would increase voting numbers and create a more 'United' Kingdom, with a more broad political spectrum. As well as more political parties to choose from!

The subject of Sex Education in schools has been a subject that has become more prominent in recent times, with some primary schools opting to teach primary school students, not only the ins and outs of the human body, but also the ins and outs of gender fluency and sexual orientation. I believe we forget these are kids, kids people!

There main concern should be what they want for breakfast, can they go play in the park? Will my mum or dad get me that toy I want?? Not..Do I like boys or girls? Do I identify as a male or female or neither!!! This is too much information which they cannot and should not be expected to process at that age. It's immoral and cruel to place that kind of expectation and information upon them.

I would pass legislation to only teach the basic principles of Sex Education in primary schools, which is what has been happening in primary schools for decades prior to this.

It is however, very important to teach our children about the LGBTQ+ community, however this should be taught in secondary schools, year 10 onwards. This means pupils would be at an age where they will have a sense of maturity to start learning these options and what they mean.

Until then, let kids be kids.

So I decided next to tackle our embarrassing apprenticeship system. The system that, instead of identifying and implementing for themselves, what I propose here, our political powerheads have decided to dilute the apprenticeship uptake figures by creating joke apprenticeships. This only allows for Companies and Corporations, to underpay the public for unskilled positions once completed. i.e. 'Apprentice Retail Assistant'. I mean you're joking right?

Our government has introduced this so they can shout 'Hey! We have boosted apprenticeships by 30%!! Look how good we are!!' This is rubbish and don't believe a word of it.

It is no coincidence apprenticeships have risen, but the amount of skilled workers/tradesmen have fallen. This is a prime example of political point scoring, over economic prosperity.

This apprenticeship system requires reform. Having fallen victim to the deficiencies of this system, this is an issue close to my heart.

Let me tell you my story.

When I left school, there was nothing more I wanted then to become a Plumber, like my grandfather. I had passed my GCSE's and had made it successfully onto the course.

Unfortunately, my dear grandfather had already passed away by this time, so I needed a plumber, who I had no connection with to take me on as their apprentice.

I was living in Bristol at the time, being a fairly big and bustling city, I did not think this would be a hardship..boy was I wrong.

I was determined to make my dream a reality. So, I sent a letter proclaiming my family history and worth and determination to every plumber and construction firm in Bristol, and I mean EVERY single one. No response.

I visited every plumber in the Phone book (for people born in the last 2 decades, this was a book delivered to every household that held every number and address in, pretty much what a Google search will do for you now) in Bristol, I got laughed at and doors slammed in my face.

What I found was a complete disinterest in taking on apprentices, this seemed to be more effort than reward for them. All I wanted was a chance to prove myself, a chance to do a profession I loved and would enjoy. I had dreams of starting my own company and building on this to create my own multi trade building firm and become beautifully rich.

As I continued my search, I saw more and more of my classmates continuing on the course, these did so because they had family members in the trade. I did not have this. My grandfather was dead, my dad was a Trade Union regional secretary, my mother a nurse, both very good professions, but not ones that would help me.

This spelt the end of my dream. All I wanted was to acquire a trade for myself, start a business and gradually an empire, all whilst doing something I enjoyed.
I was forced to quit the course and was left wandering in the wilderness.

This should not happen. Full stop.

I believe we should create a system where we have local trades people tied to a college, so work placements are available to all. The trades people would be reimbursed for doing this, via a non-taxable annual payment scheme.

This would create an incentive to entice trades people to take on apprentices. This will in turn, increase the skills market and boost the economy.

No more broken dreams, just opportunities and growth.

Now, having being left in the wilderness, I then went on to work several meaning less jobs, earning money but gaining no skills other than customer service and a great deal of patience!

It's in this instance that I looked at the adult learning courses that were available. There were huge varieties, but not many that seemed to provide me with a useful qualification at the end of it. The ones that did do this, you had to pay for, and pay a lot for. For someone being paid minimum wage and renting, this made my options few. So I continued on, existing, let down by the system, again. A system, that I seemed to be paying more and more taxes for, making it increasingly unlikely I would get the opportunity anyway.

This is why I would increase the variety of available *Free* Adult Learning Courses, that provide key skills, to fill key areas and provide you with a valuable qualification at the end of it.

A stepping stone

We have recently had the announcement by Rishi Sunak about implementing mandatory national service.

I was, and I don't think I was alone on this, very taken aback. I was quickly transported to a World War 2 era! We suddenly seemed to be on a war footing.

Now, after the initial shock died down, this started making more and more sense. At the same time, it made less and less sense on how it was being delivered to the nation.

National service does have its benefits, it *would* create a stronger sense of national pride and community. It *would* also put us on a better footing, should the worst happen, following the invasion of Ukraine.

However, I do not think we can now justify implementing this in the fashion it has been proposed and restricting the freedom of our more liberal and free youth. This should only be called upon should and ONLY if, the worst did happen and the western world and democracy is once again threatened.

But there is a need for a format of national service to be implemented, for all the benefits mentioned before.

So I would introduce ' National Service Weeks'… Tah Dah!!

This suggestion is a lot more palatable for the public and myself. Instead of deploying a mandatory national service, as proposed, include 'National Service Weeks' to our curriculum. This *could* even be during the summer holidays, when a variety of summer clubs take place.

Similar to work experience weeks, this gives students the opportunity to experience what life would be like in the Armed Forces and Emergency Services, to entice more applicants and boost numbers in the future.

They will get to experience the comradery that you get in the forces and emergency services. It would give students a greater respect for these roles and everything that is involved in it and no doubt inspire the next generation.

This in short, does everything Rishi wants, without restricting young people's liberty.

# THE
# WELFARE
## SYSTEM

---

As we know the current welfare system is *not* sustainable. It does not work….fact. It is easily abused and manipulated and this abundant misuse creates a huge financial deficit and stops the system working for those who *actually* need it. So how would I change it?

By applying the following rules:

**Any new applicants post April 2025, will need to be born in the United Kingdom or hold a valid UK Passport for a least 5 years, this would need to be evidenced at the time of applying.**

**Set up a new department, named 'Welfare Audit Department', whose purpose is to look at existing claimants and review what is currently being claimed and set in motion action plans, if applicable, to support the return of applicants to work where possible.**

**Increase prison terms/penalties for benefit fraud to act as a deterrent.**

**Change the current position of only offering monetary benefits and include instead Food Vouchers, Energy and Water Allowances, Childcare Vouchers, in turn reducing the monetary offering given.**

**Continue to cap Child Tax Credits/Universal Credit at two children.**

**Completely stop Child Benefit payments for Higher Rate Tax payers.**

**Reinstate Legal Aid for lower income households.**

Our welfare system has supported our population for decades when we find ourselves out of work or unable to. Unfortunately, this system is being abused more and more, with what seems to be, *no* auditors or not enough, to check claims to see if they are genuine.

For example, I read a news story recently where a Bulgarian gang had immigrated across to the United Kingdom and had started to create fake identities and using these identities to claim more benefits. This went on for almost 5 years before they were caught. They managed to accumulate millions and I mean *millions* of pounds of tax payers money. They managed to acquire enough money in fact, to rebuild their home town back in Bulgaria.

We have to question, how bad is our system for them to get away with it for so long?

Do we not have a team in place that audits claims?

We clearly do not request enough, or the right kind of evidence upon submission of these claims.

This example is just one of many examples of the abuse of the system put in place to help people. This is why I propose to create a new department to audit claims and update what evidence is required and create a more secure submission process.

This way if we can stop the abuse of the system, it will begin to stabilise and would create wealth to be able to use elsewhere.

We do also have to recognise that the system is overwhelmed, it is simply too expensive to fund. Which means no matter how we audit it or who looks at it, cuts need to be made to bring about stability and affordability.

To begin with, I would bring in force a requirement for all new claimants to be born in the United Kingdom or hold a valid UK Passport for at least 5 years. This would need to be evidenced at the time, with a face to face meeting required annually.

As a deterrent, harsher punishments should be brought into force against benefit fraud, including longer prison terms.

I believe we should change how benefits are offered also, in place of pure monetary benefits, I would replace 60% of this, with Food Vouchers and energy & water grants.

I would also increase free childcare amounts from 15 hours to 25 hours to help break the prison of benefits. It should never be more beneficial to claim benefits than work.

Now, we must also put a limit on things, I've seen firsthand, the mums that are so work shy, they prefer to have another child to delay the return to work, rather than start working for their money. They tend to also be working 'cash in hand' jobs at the same time. These people are claiming tax payers money, but are buying Botox and going on luxury holidays. I would say, not the best use of a strained welfare system.

If you want to work 'cash in hand' jobs, I say fair play to you! Just please stop spending *my* money.

When I see 20% disappear from my hard earned pay packet and then I see a 'Kelly' down the road going on a 2nd holiday to Spain not having worked a single day in 6 years, I want to scream 'just stop spending my money please! Make your own!'.

Please note: I am not tarnishing the name Kelly, this was purely random.

I would completely stop Child Benefit for Higher rate tax payers. I mean they don't *need* it, it should be a system to support the average tax payer and if you are paying a higher rate of tax, that's not average. This would generate significant funds to support other causes.

And lastly, I would reinstate *free* legal aid. This was a lifeline to me in my early twenties and I will tell you why.

When I was at school I met, who I thought, would be the love of my life. We dated each other on and off for 3 or 4 years, before we made it official and I moved out of my parents' house to live with her. We got married and had a child, my first son. We had an extremely volatile relationship, my wife was not pleasant to me, I suffered what can only be described as emotional abuse at the hands of her.

One cold and rainy night, it all came to a head and I left, with my son crying in my partners arms.

This was one of the hardest decisions in my life, but I knew 100% it was the right one. I had to start thinking of my son, and the environment he would eventually grow up in.

I didn't want him to grow up in house where his parents were constantly at each other's throats. I wanted him to grow up in a loving household, a stable household. So I left.

What happened after this was the hardest two years of my life.

My ex-wife had decided she didn't want me to be a part of my son's life and refused to let me see him. She would call me up saying 'He doesn't know who you are anyway so why bother? Stay away'.

As you can imagine, this was distressing and heartbreaking not only for me, a first time dad, but for my family, first time grandparents, uncles, aunties.

So I went to a solicitor in Bristol and we got nowhere for 1 and half years. I saw my son in 10 minute slots and sometimes not for months.

Then I moved down to Exeter with my parents and got a new solicitor. He looked at my case and said 'enough is enough, it's time for court'.

We went through a 6 month court case, where my ex-wife tried every trick in the book to stop me from seeing my son. To paint a picture of the situation and my ex-wife's cruelty and stubbornness, her solicitor approached me and my solicitor to apologise for her behaviour and to say he is 'pleading' with her to settle the case.

Although our relationship was volatile, and I played my part in that, I did not for one instance think the person I believed would be my partner for life, could be capable of such cruelty. I know that if I had the main custody of our son, I would of *never* of stopped his mother from seeing him.

Eventually, the court ordered that I could see my son regularly. I got to see my son on the weekend, every two weeks and a week in the holidays. We even managed to negotiate that I could have him every other Christmas. I had won.

This would not of been possible if I did not have legal aid available to me. There is not a chance I would have been able to afford the solicitor fees. I would not of been a part of my sons life, he would not have known me or my family.

I know for a fact I am not the only person that has been in that position. I hate to think of the position of the dads now, that cannot see their children due to someone else's selfishness and no help being available to battle it.

This aid *must* be a permanent feature, I owe it a great deal and it is pivotal to thousands of single parent families out there, that are missing out on a relationship with their children.

# TAXES

Not going to lie, this is a difficult topic. In one hand, I would love to go full on 'Liz Truss' mode and cut everything, everywhere, but as we know, this leads to market instability and a lot of resignations! I think in this instance, a more cautious approach is required.

**I would freeze the lower and higher rate tax bands for 3 years, to help reduce national debt after which, the lower rate tax band will increase to £13,250. The higher tax band will remain frozen.**

**I would lower the Corporation Tax rate to the pre 23/24 rate of 19% to attract more business from big firms.**

**I would introduce a 'Tourist Tax' of £3 - £7 per night per person, to be applied to England, this would be optional for the devolved governments.**

**I would lower tax duty on alcohol sold in pubs to boost the industry.**

**Scrap inheritance tax, this should of never been implemented in the first place!**

**Increase Tax on nicotine products (excluding nicotine cessation aids) by 20%, to stop the increase of 'Vape' usage, to work towards a smoke free Britain.**

**I would create 'Legal Task Force' to look at existing legislation to close the legal 'loop holes' that allow for tax evasion.**

I would scrap the Non Dom status, if you live in the UK for more than 3 months of the year, you will pay tax the same as everyone else in the UK.

I would introduce a lower rate of tax of 15% (lower) for the Armed Forces (excluding reserves) and Emergency Services (excluding reserves).

So, taxes, where do I start? We need to start getting a control of this, to improve people's lives. How we perform in the other topics covered, very much determines what you can do. So you need to perform at every other level, to affect anything on this level.

I would begin by freezing the lower tax band and higher rate tax bands for around 3 years to reduce the national debt. Having been in debt myself, I know how essential it is that we pay a good portion of that off. After the 3 years I would increase the tax band to £13,250, this would provide an extra £400 a year in the average workers' pay packet.

I would lower Corporation Tax, that's right, lower it! Because you need to attract big businesses to boost economic growth and achieve a healthy economy. The sooner we can attract these businesses, the more jobs there will be, the more investment and general wealth.

The big one! I would introduce a tourist tax, this is so simple, I cannot believe we do not already do it!

Spain do it, Italy do it, this is lost revenue, which we sorely need. This will brings us in line with most of Europe and it would generate a revenue of £737 million to £1 billion per year (based on the average tourists numbers to visit United Kingdom, 35.1 million, staying for 7 nights). I mean come on! It's a no brainer. This would generate plenty of funds to invest in other areas.

We have all seen a decline in the pub industry over the years, first covid, then the cost of living. It has now become cheaper to drink at home than go out to a pub. Considerably cheaper. This needs to change if we want the industry to survive. Which is why I recommend a decrease in tax duty for alcohol sold in public houses and restaurants, to be able to pass this down to the customer and boost the struggling industry.

I would scrap inheritance tax straight away, it is not even remotely fair to tax someone on the gift left behind by their loving departed family. It is the very last present a parent can give to their children, their grandchildren. Why the hell are we taxing that? Delete! Gone!

We live in a society now where for the first time, we could actually become smoke free.

Cigarettes, Cigars etc, are on their way out in the UK and that can be nothing but good news.

You may find it strange to hear I love smoking, *love* it! I started smoking when I was 13 years old, and did so until I was 30. Even now and then I find myself having a cheeky one.

But you cannot hide from the fact they are bad for you in every way. They not only cause cancer, but several other conditions and diseases.

It being an addiction, we need a push in the right direction, so a 20% tax rise should do it!

This will stop the increase of our younger population taking up vaping, the effects of which, we *actually* do not yet know fully.

Vapes are cheap and full of nicotine, so let's increase the price, to make them unaffordable for our young people.

At the same time we need to offer cheaper smoking cessation products.

Let's go for it and become healthier! It will further reduce the burden on the National Health Service, among general health and financial benefits. Win win!

Now, we can make all of these proposals, which in theory would be perfect and bring the plan together. The key objective, which every plan on taxes hinges on, is people *actually* paying them. There are currently too many loop holes (sometimes purposedly put there) to avoid this.

If every company and wealthier individual decided to do the right thing and pay the full amount of tax they are meant to be paying, this would bring an additional staggering figure of £1.8 billion into the economy.

What effects could an extra £1.8 billion have to our social care, National Health Service and our tax rate?

Instead these people decide to use offshore accounts, over claim on expenses, use non domicile statuses – scrapping this too by the way! For what purpose? An additional yacht?

But don't get me wrong, this is not all companies, this is not everyone who is wealthy. You will find companies and wealthy people who are the most generous people you will know and we should *never* taint all people by the actions of a few.

As we mentioned in the welfare chapter, the same type of people exist on the other side of the wealth divide.

What we must do is tighten up legislation and increase punishment terms to stop and deter this from happening. This is why I would put together a non-biased, independent legal team to put this in place.

Don't get me wrong, if I was in government, I think I would probably struggle to get this policy past the line. There are too many MPs serving their own interests to let this one pass!

One thing that is abundantly clear, we need more of the population to want to work for our key services. It simply is not worth it financially to do this currently.

Yes the pension maybe good, but I have worked for a few corporations where it is better. This is not enough to attract and keep dedicated employees. It needs to be worth it financially.

It astounds me how the salary offered for National Health Service and Armed Forces roles, has not increased in line with the times.

Take for example, my mother. She studied for four years to gain her nursing degree and then worked a further twenty plus years to reach the top of her salary band, which was £35,000 a year.

I left school with a handful of GCSEs and worked for a corporation as a Customer Service Assistant and started on that, within a year I was earning more than that, with commission on top.

Now you explain to me, why would I want to spend four years studying, racking up thousands of pounds of debt in university fees, to then have to work decades to reach a pay level, which someone with no experience, uneducated, can walk into a easier job with less responsibility and earn the same? You wouldn't....and that is the problem.

Why are we reliant on oversea workers to fill NHS jobs? Because it is low paid work. Cheap labour.

How do you fix it now it is more difficult to obtain cheap labour? Well, I am by no means a rocket scientist, but - pay more?

It seems so simple, but our politicians seem to not want to go there. You want a stable National Health Service? Invest in it!

When I say invest, I don't mean add another manager or increase the pay of the director. No, I mean pay its workers more. From the cleaners, to the doctors. Pay more. Make it more attractive. Pay the people that care for your loved ones what they are worth.
These people deal with trauma we would never want to see, then they go home and can't afford the weekly shop. It's simply wrong.
Our armed forces, go to hostile environments and risk their very lives to make people safe. We need them, they are essential. They are as we heard continuously during covid, *key* workers.
So I would to start with, having a reduced tax rate for all key workers. I myself would happily accept these workers having a better tax rate for the service they provide for us all.
Let's fill our services with skilled and *looked after* workers and furthermore, let's keep them!

# THE

# NATIONAL
# HEALTH
## SERVICE

---

Now, as we touched on previously, our NHS is not in a good state and drastic measures are required to try and increase efficiency and stability.

Here's what I would propose:

**Streamline current management structure to reduce costs and create a more effective system. The end result would be reduced management numbers and an increase in Nurses and Doctors.**

**Introduce the lower tax rate (15%) for Emergency Services.**

**Implement a 5% Salary Increase.**

**Scrap all parking charges for NHS employees.**

**NHS to be made free of charge after holding a UK passport for three years for people whose country of birth is not in the UK – National Insurance Number required if above age 16.**

**Conduct a review of NHS offerings to remove any unnecessary procedures.**

**Each hospital to conduct waiting list review to prioritise procedures in a case by case basis.**

**Government grants for UK passport holders residing in England to pay 20% towards course fees for nursing and medical qualifications.**

We as a nation should be proud of our National Health Service. It is the greatest free healthcare system in the world. It is a service that is admired around the globe and with good cause.

It is because of this service many of us are able to live healthy, longer lives.

But this service is at risk, its waiting lists are enormous, it's workers under paid and unhappy. More and more it's doctors are moving over to the private sector and who can blame them.

This service has been mismanaged for so long, it is quickly becoming unreliable and unbelievably inefficient. It is making more and more mistakes and in some hospitals, they are stretched so thin on the ground, it is becoming dangerous.

If you speak to several specialists on this subject, they all say the same thing, it needs more investment and a reorganisation.

If you work for a decent length of time in any organisation, there is normally a general reorganisation and streamlining of the management structure, every three to four years. When was the last time this happened in the NHS? Instead of streamlining services, we make them more convoluted.

We need to remove management where it is not needed, disband boards where there doesn't need to be one and streamline the service so it is more efficient and effective. This way we can free up funds to invest in its workers and its equipment and facilities. To adhere to minimum staffing levels.
As mentioned before, we need to attract new skilled workers to the service, by making it worthwhile financially. To do this we would provide a pay increase and a lower tax rate. We need to further provide grants for university fees for key skills.

We can pay for this by streamlining services and recouping tax from tax avoidance and the introduction of the tourist tax.

We need to make this more stable and reduce the strain on the service by only making it available to people whose country of birth is outside of the UK, *after* they have held a UK passport for 3 years. This is not a harsh policy to bring into force, but a fair one.

We need to look at what procedures and services are offered on the NHS for free, as there are some, which simply should not be free. Liposuction and tummy tucks amongst them.

Though very important for some patients, these procedures are not essential and should be private.

I recently had Lasik eye laser surgery, this to me was life changing. I would love for it to available on the NHS. I know however, this is not essential, it will not reduce my life expectancy if I didn't get it done. So rightfully it's private. We need to paint other procedures with the same brush and redirect those resources to essential operations.

We need to make it abundantly clear to GP's to increase face to face appointments.

To reiterate the importance of this, I will tell you of a terrible story, which demonstrates the cost of getting this wrong.

A perfectly healthy man in his thirties, started complaining to his partner about an ear ache and was worried about lumps on his neck.
He rang his local GP, and was given a time slot for a telephone appointment. Not face to face. After speaking to his GP they

recommended paracetamol and assured him, they did not think it was serious, even though they never saw him in person.

This ear ache did not go away, he had in total four remote consultations, each time being reassured that he was fine, without ever seeing him in person.

As each phone call happened, his symptoms got worse. He started getting blood in his urine, the doctor said this was a urine infection. He called again, complaining of a fever and neck pain, the doctor said this was a 'flu' like illness and prescribed pain relief for his neck pain.

What they did not know, which they would of if seen in person, was this man had developed an abscess on his brain stem, that was triggered by an inner ear infection.

He died two days after the last call.

This was a death caused by a system that was not functioning.

My own grandmother died in a hospital toilet whilst waiting to be seen for over 5 hours in an A&E waiting room.

There are countless stories like these, which could have been prevented. Lives that could have been saved, but were let down by an over stretched, underfunded and mismanaged service.

# IMMIGRATION

We cannot continue to accommodate the vast number of people coming in to the UK and believe that society will still function, it will not.

Therefore, radical changes are required:

**Introduce a complete halt to new asylum claims.**

**Continue the Rwanda policy proposed by the Conservatives.**

**For legal immigration, the applicant must have an essential skill or be a qualified professionals with a position of employment already confirmed.**

**They must have at least £10,000 in a bank account or savings account.**

**The welfare system and NHS will be unavailable to new immigrants until they have resided in the UK for at least 3 years (from issue date of UK passport).**

**The restrictions on this system will include housing, no housing will be offered to illegal or legal immigrants.**

Review the financial agreement with France to deter illegal crossings, to include penalties for crossings made from across the channel.

Invest in more staffing for the Immigration enforcement department, to root out employers taking on illegal immigrants.

This is the subject which makes people feel the most uncomfortable to talk about. Taboo, almost. But it should not be.

It should be made plain and clear from the off, at no point are any of these policies influenced by prejudice or any form of hate or discrimination.

This is purely based on realism. Facts, maths and nothing else.
Now immigration can be both a positive and a negative. We need it, as much as needing less of it. But one thing is certain, we need to control it.

What we need to remember, is that although our hearts are enormous, our country is not.

Let me put this into perspective, you can fit the UK into Australia 31 times, USA – 40 times. We are not a big country, these countries mentioned have tougher immigration rules than we currently do.

The increase in the number of people to live in the UK alone, not just referring to illegal immigration, has increased significantly and our infrastructure and environment cannot and *will* not cope if it continues.

The NHS will become to stretched and ineffective and broken, the welfare system will need to be reduced or scrapped and the impact on the environment will be devastating. This is not scare mongering, this is starting to *already* happen and it would take stringent measures to be put in place to be able to stabilise the current situation.
This is something we cannot do, if we do not face up to the facts. Not everyone who wants tougher rules in place on immigration

and tighter restrictions and access to the NHS and benefit systems are racist and hold prejudice, it is simply untrue. This unfortunately, is what you are branded as by celebrities and main stream media should you deem to have an opinion that is different to theirs.

We are meant to be living in a country of free will and speech, but this could not be further from the truth.

In the past 20 years our ability to speak freely has become *so* restricted, it has impacted our politics, community, even our entertainment. I have seen people express their opinions and it be deemed controversial, 'against the grain', and they have lost their jobs and become social pariahs. It's complete madness.

Though deemed unpopular, the Conservatives Rwanda Policy is the current best option on the table. This policy would deter people making illegal crossings, knowing they are only going to be deported to Rwanda once crossed.  This will deter them from risking their lives and the lives of their children, in a needless journey that is costing so many.

No matter how much in our hearts, we would like to believe we could crush a global people smuggling ring that has been operating for decades, it is not possible, to tackle the gangs head on, as suggested by Labour.

If by some impressive global operation you manage to remove one gang, another will take its place. We would have as much success with that, as we did attempting to remove the Taliban from Afghanistan. Twice.

The only way to deter this mass illegal smuggling ring, is to make the destination unavailable. Other nations know this, which is why they are adopting the similar policies.

We would then need to put in place a more stringent criteria for people wanting to legally immigrate to the UK. Such as having an essential skill or be a qualified professional with secure employment already acquired, this in turn can be documented and audited. They would need to have at least £10,000 in a bank or savings account, this is a similar policy as what Canada imposes.

This would ensure when they make the move across to the UK, they have enough saved to hit the ground running, this would also ensure they have enough saved to obtain private medical insurance.

This would be required for 3 years, after which the NHS and welfare system would be available.

I would for the purposes of maintaining our green belt and stabilising house prices, stop housing via the welfare system being available to all illegal or legal immigrants.

As mentioned before, we are a small country, and we cannot continue to build houses and slowly eat up our countryside.

The UK is known as one of the most nature *depleted* countries in the world as a result of the continual drive to build more houses.

Species of animals in the UK have declined by 19% since the 1970's.
Now nearly 1 in 6 species (16.1%) are now threatened with extinction.

We cannot keep building houses to accommodate an influx in immigration, as well as natural population increase.

It is not sustainable. Fact. Not racism. Not prejudice. Just facts.

Now, I would not begin to lay the blame solely on immigration for this, this is also to do with how we farm our land, the processes we use and other environmental factors, but it does play its part.

I would also review the financial agreement we have with France and the EU to stop illegal immigration. £500 million? Is this money well spent? As the effect seems to be minimal. I do believe we need to have cooperation to tackle the issue. But are we doing this in the most effective way?

If we have the Rwanda policy in force, do we need to pay France for a detention centre in their country and extra workers? We could in fact purpose, we pay for it, staff it and control it.

Or if the Rwanda policy is effective, we would not need it, as they would be deported upon arrival.

I am sceptical about the effort put in by our European neighbours to stop migrants coming across. I would at least conduct a deep review on the practices employed to deter crossings and the effectiveness of them, to see if it is essentially 'worth the money'.

We could redirect that money into our own border force and immigration department.

This would create more capability to also root out employers taking on illegal immigrants, who are normally treated horrendously and end up, in what is essentially slavery.

The conditions these people are subject to, are incomprehensible. They are paid a pittance and kept in squalor. All for a profit.

Once we tackle the gangs and employers in *our* country that facilitate this appalling trade, this will also reduce illegal immigration and the destruction of lives.

There we have it! That wasn't too painful. If I have offended you, please, please, please remember.

I don't care.

# UK AID

---

Conduct a formal review of Foreign Aid being offered.

Remove countries with strong growing economies.

Review and construct aid plans to help self enhancement by providing technology and infrastructure recommendations.

Maintain the level of GDP currently spent on Foreign Aid.

I am a strong believer that we in the UK, have a responsibility to do what we can to help the poorer countries around the world. Not only the UK, but all high-income developed countries. We can only solve the problems of hunger and poverty by working together and giving what we can.

However, we need to ensure this is provided to countries struggling financially, whose people are effected by poverty and whose countries are doing what they can to tackle these issues.

We should *not* be providing aid to countries whose people are suffering, but they take no action on this and instead push on with policies and schemes that are only beneficial to themselves. Throwing money to these countries, will only fill the pockets of the people and governments that are causing the problems.

With these countries, we should instead be sharing technology on infrastructure, propose solutions to help combat the issues facing them, so they themselves can put plans into place to help strengthen their communities and economies. But it has to be something *they* implement, as just chucking money at a problem never solves it.

There are certain countries such as India, that we provide aid to, who instead of tackling poverty, have decided to prioritise running their own space program. This is a fault with the governments priorities, rather than their finances.

In this instance, it is such a horrendous misuse of taxpayers money to provide self-sufficient countries, with monetary aid.

We need to conduct a review of what countries receive aid and in what form, to see if this is providing the right type of aid. I would aim to keep the level of UK Aid frozen and consistent.

# ENERGY

# &

# WATER

---

The current price of energy is astronomical, as we know this has been driven up by the war in Ukraine, but also highlighted the dependency on fossil fuels provided by less than favourable countries. We have learned from this experience that this method cannot continue.

Here is what I would propose.

**Construct 3 new nuclear power sites in England.**

**Invest further in Wind and Hydro power sites.**

**Lower the Energy Price Cap considerably, based on the energy companies profits for the year, to allow for a reduction in energy costs to be passed to the consumer, rather than considerable increased profits.**

**Create a new NATO style energy pact with global democracies to promote an equal energy market. This will provide security during crisis and strengthen diplomatic ties.**

**Invest in further research, collaborating with global democracies on new renewable energy sources.**

**Create a salary and bonus cap for energy firm executives.**

**Increase penalties, to include prison terms, for unauthorised illegal sewage dumping.**

We have never as a nation experienced energy issues, in the post war era as we do today.

Of course, Russia's actions in Ukraine have played an enormous role in this and have laid bare the fragility of our energy market, and also the corruption.

This has opened the eyes of the western world, of the reliance we have on Russian oil and gas. It has prompted us to look at different methods to stop this reliance.

We need to look at more state owned sustainable methods of obtaining energy. We should commission a further 3 nuclear power stations to help provide energy to the United Kingdom.

We should look to obtain new contracts with democratic nations to provide our gas supplies.

We need to invest in more high tech Hydro and Wind power sites to start moving away from fossil fuels and invest further in research on this.

With this in mind, we need to create a new NATO style energy pact. This will help regulate energy companies across the western world to ensure a fairer consumer price and stability in the market. In times of most need, we have seen the CEOs and shareholders of these energy firms pocket billions, at the expense of the general public.

This would also provide security, when crisis like the Ukraine war happen. How can we defend a democratic society against a tyrant when we are so reliant on its resources? This cannot happen again.

Working together on renewable energy sources, technology can be shared and distributed on a global scale.

What can I say about the water companies? Let's start with this.

In 2023, waters companies spent 3.6 million hours spilling sewage into our rivers and seas.

This is up from 1.75 million hours in 2022.

With this all happening in the background, you be pleased to know that since the last general election, water company bosses have paid themselves £25 million in bonuses and incentives.

This is when most of the south coast, has had warnings against swimming, due to polluted waters. But that doesn't concern these criminals, as they have just paid themselves enough money to travel to tropical waters, and live there, for the rest of their lives!

Only 14% of the rivers in England can currently claim to be free from chemical contamination.

How are they getting away with this? Why are they not held to account? These are failures that put people's health at risk and instead of financial penalties, they are receiving financial rewards?

This is why I would implement financial penalties and punishments against these CEO's, that continue to operate with negligence and a complete disregard to human safety.

A dramatic change is required to resolve the situation, I would prefer to see the running of something so pivotal as our water supply to be solely in the hands of the state, as it is a critical part of our infrastructure. Though I admit, I cannot begin to imagine the cost of this, but does that outweigh the cost of clean water? Healthy rivers and seas with increased biodiversity?

At least if we are keeping this sector private, cannot we not sack the current contractors for poor performance? Isn't that what is done in almost every other industry?

Kick out the corrupt ineffective companies and replace these with reputable ones.

# PENSIONS

It seems the state pension is getting further and further out of our grasps.

So I would propose the following:

**Reduce the state pension retirement age to 60.**

**I would increase the required years of National Insurance contributions to 40, to be able to receive the Full Rate.**

**Less than 35 years of National Insurance contributions would be lower rate.**

**To counter act the cost of an earlier retirement age, I would freeze the pension increase each year to 2%**

**I would reintroduce the Bus Pass for over 60's.**

**I would make pension monthly payments non-taxable.**

The retirement age has increased to 66, with talks of a further increase to 70! It will eventually come to the point where the majority of us will be to old and immobile, to be able to fully enjoy the pension that has been hard earned or we would of popped our clogs before we get to it! I mean, what is the actual point of the pension if it was to start at 70? That is a lot of tax being paid, for extremely little return.

I do not think I would be alone in saying this has to be reduced, though we would love to retire at the age of 40, I'd say 60 is a sensible age for this to start. This obviously would have to be paid for, so it would be a case of changing the National Insurance contributions requirement and freezing the increase of pension payouts to 2%.

This would ensure those people that have paid the most during their lifetimes get the maximum pay outs, which is only fair.

Also, why do we supply bus passes for over 60's to Scotland and Northern Ireland, but not England and Wales? (Except of course London). This should be nationwide, I would bring this back in straight away and make this equal across the United Kingdom.

We should not be applying tax on state pension payments, as this money is generated from tax payments. Why are we re-taxing something that has already been taxed? This seems immoral to me.

That's essentially awarding Tax Credits or Universal Credit and then taxing people on it!

# POLICE

---

We have all seen a depleted police presence (except London) and seen anti-social behaviour increase.

Here is what I would do to change this:

**Increase police numbers by a target of 25,000.**

**Implement a new specific directive to increase police presence on the street, in all districts.**

**A review to be conducted into police training and refined DBS checks and psychological profiling to be conducted as part of the recruitment process.**

**Stop and search powers increased, with each officer to be carrying body cameras, to protect both officer and civilian.**

**Increase in educational visits to schools and colleges to raise awareness of current issues and promote recruitment.**

**Fitness tests to be conducted annually and standards increased.**

Now it always amazes me when you hear in the media 'Anti-social behaviour is on the rise!' or 'Crime rate increases' and 'People feeling unsafe on the streets'.

What do you expect? If you drastically cut police funding and in short, police numbers, the issues the police are their to deter and prevent are going to increase. Seems pretty logical to me.

I know when I was younger, I was born in the 80's by the way, so not too long ago! You would always have a police presence in your town centre, and local area. This acted as a deterrent and helped stop anti-social behaviour, like pub closing time scraps. Just a presence of the law, will always make potential trouble makers think twice. It brought you peace of mind that you were safe, safe to walk home after dark.

They have taken this away, and as soon as you do this, the only thing that will fill its place, is unlawfulness.

Just having additional police officers would reduce knife crime and gang violence which is on the rise.

But this does go hand in hand with giving our police officers the power and confidence, to be able to prevent these crimes from happening.

How can we expect our officers to enforce the law if they are in constant threat of disciplinary action?
If they go to search someone and that person proclaims abuse or prejudice, you can be sure it is the officer that will be penalised. If not doing so already, I would make it mandatory for all officers to wear body cams. This would prevent unfair persecution, with that in place there is no reason to not increase the search and stops powers currently given.

51

I cannot see how this would do anything but reduce knife crime and counter act the drug trade?

Do not get me wrong, you need to be able to have confidence in our police force. We have had a few instances where the very service that is meant to protect you, turn out to be the very people that will cause you harm.

When you hear of these instances, the same story always ends up being told, that the officer in question had a "*history*". There had been "*warnings*".

Then you ask yourself, these people are in a position of power, in position of trust, if they have a "*history*", then they need to find another vocation. It is not penalising people for having a criminal past, it is upholding the reputation of the police force, the very system that maintains law and order in the country.

These instances have been to many of late, so I would conduct a thorough review of police training, DBS checks and psychological profiling to ensure these are as robust as possible and any "*history*" and I mean *any*, then they cannot qualify for a position.

I would put this in place for any job role that includes having responsibility of people's lives.

We also need to set people on the right path from the very beginning, when I was at school, we had a visit from Peter Andre, but not the police force. Just doing school visits to highlight the latest issues, to detail what the police force does on a day to day basis will bring more awareness to our young people, who if growing up in not the best environments, are vulnerable to manipulation.

This would also boost recruitment. Let kids see the police car, wear the hat, see the badge. If they start thinking, 'this is cool!', 'I want to be a police officer when I'm older!' They will leave with more respect for the authorities and want to join them.

On my last point, I would make sure fitness tests are annual.

There is a background to this, I used to managed a well known high street brand's store. As with any store on the high street, you get your light fingered friends, who have decided today is a 'I'm not gonna pay day', in all fairness that is normally a 'I'm not gonna pay *year*'.

This got to the extent where we needed a police presence at the store. The officer in question, was the nicest person you could hope to meet, but in terms of fitness, if someone wanted to steal something, they were getting away with it!

There was not a chance this officer was chasing, and the thief in question, did get away with it, several times. Was this person chased? Nope! But they did try to track them down in their car.

I think as a minimum requirement a basic fitness test should be required. We don't need G.I Joes, just not Homer Simpsons.

# DEFENCE

Living in the times that we do, with the war in Ukraine, increasing tensions with China and rumbles in the middle east, the threat to democracy has never been greater. Our armed forces are not equipped or big enough to protect us if required, which is now, with the threat of Russia, becoming an increasingly big worry.

Here is what I would do to change that.

**We would need to increase Defence spend to 2.5% of GDP.**

**Increase armed forces numbers to 250,000.**

**Increase recruitment for reserve forces.**

**Increase joint NATO military training exercises to deepen military and foreign alliances.**

**Increase the size of the UK naval fleet.**

**Increase the size of the UKs Air Force, including drones.**

**Pay increase and tax cut for all armed forces.**

Needless to say, the current situation with Russia and in particular Putin, has brought every western nations defence situation in to focus. Governments across the western world are reviewing their defence spend, their military alliances and increasing the size of their armed forces, and rightly so.

Russia's or more rightly *Putin's* war against Ukraine, has given the western world a reminder of what a totalitarian regime with an unstable dictator at the helm is capable of.

We cannot for one moment believe, that if or once Putin has finished his mission in Ukraine that he will stop there. He has only one thing on his mind and that is the reformation of the Soviet Union.

He, like many of his kind before him, have no care of the lives they chuck away to achieve their goals.

Putin has understood the weakness that democracy can sometimes bring about, I'm talking about complacency, an inability to prioritise doing the right thing over profits and the economy, and a severe lack of staying power.

Putin knows to win this war, all he needs to do is hold out. Wait for the western worlds patience to run out. He knows that we could ultimately defeat his forces if we were to join them and help defend Ukraine, but knows the likelihood is that we will not. We will not risk open warfare, which would most certainly lead to a third world war. No one wants that.

So all he has to do, is wait. Eventually, the western powers will get tired of funding a war which has essentially no end, our resolve will weaken and the people of the western world will turn against its leaders until we decide to stop helping. It is at that point the war will end, for Ukraine.

For Putin, he will continue his crusade across the Baltic States to continue his pursuit of past glories, these battles no doubt, will be also started under the false pretence of a noble war to root out prejudice.

What we are unsure of, is what we will accept. At what point do we decide we need to step in, in other ways than just supplying arms and enforcing sanctions, which it seems all of Russia's wealthiest people, had been preparing for. They are, by some strange coincidence, still rich.

This has been a war in the making for quite some time. Putin first tested the waters to gauge the reaction of the western world by invading Crimea. What did we do? Impose a few sanctions and then forgot about it. There's those predictable democratic weaknesses, complacency.

Straight away, Putin would be thinking, great! So all I have to do to prepare is sure up my economy to survive sanctions, create partnerships with other pariah nations and we are good to go.

He starts his war and it seems to take an age for the western world to react, though we can be proud to say Boris Johnson was a bit more proactive than his predecessor David Cameron, and spear headed the effort and rhetoric in opposing Putin. This was not what Putin was expecting.

We have since managed to remove what was a strong prime minister on the global stage, to replace them with leaders that have no agenda, other than their own political gains. Putin must of thought 'That is that problem solved!'.

Though he made several mistakes and blunders, and questionable decisions, Boris Johnson was a strong leader. He brought about a majority in parliament not seen for a very long time and for me rightly or wrongly, I believe his time was cut short too soon. He was a prime minister of action, maybe not always the right action, but he took action.

Since then, everything is slowly going according to Putin's plans. The wests resolve is weakening, the first sign of this is Americas delay in the funding bill.

You can tell this, as the Ukraine war is already yesterday's news. Coverage in in main stream media is minimal. Especially with the outbreak of the Gaza conflict.

This was and is Putin's target. What we do not know, is his plans after this.

This is what we and every western nation needs to prepare for, in case we *do* decide to be more actively involved and if Putin does the unthinkable and attacks a NATO member.

That is why over the past decade, western nations have started to rev up defence spend and start schemes like 'National Service', to prepare the people of the west for the unthinkable.

We need to increase recruitment of all forces, increase our fleet and air force size. Strengthen our military alliances.

This would include reaching out to nations we have not been overly close to, like China. As a major player, it is vitally important we do what we can to make them an ally, rather than an enemy.

Like or not, Russia poses a very *real* threat, which we need to be ready for.

We also need to take care of our forces and compensate them to the value they provide. This would of course include a pay rise similar to what is proposed for the NHS and a separate tax rate of 15% instead of 20%, to attract more personnel and retain more expertise.

We also need to insure we are taking care of our veterans, with an improved welfare system this would be more possible. We would be able to invest more in our social care for veterans and provide help with housing when needed. As they have invested in us, we need to invest in them.

With the increase in defence spend, we need to spread this across all sectors, including cyber defence and to investigate any political tampering, which has become more frequent.

These are things that can be scaled down during times of peace, as we have done since WW2 and the Falklands war. But these things also need to be scaled up when our democracy and society are threatened as they are today

# THE
# HOUSE
## OF
# LORDS

One word:

*Abolish.*

I am a strong believer in tradition and ceremony, however this outdated department of unelected noble men and women, do not have a place in the more modern parliamentary system.

It is a needless expense to the taxpayer that adds no *real* value to the parliamentary system. A retirement home for ex MPS to get pocket money.

These Lords and Ladies, are unelected and for the most part unwanted. They can only serve their own interests, as they represent no one.

Put this in perspective, in the 2022/23 financial year, the costs of the House of Lords (excluding estates and non-cash items) was £104,670,000. Of that amount, costs relating directly to the Members Finance Scheme (including allowances and travel expenses) totalled £21,110,000.

Now surely, this money could be redirected towards better costs? Defence? Welfare? The NHS?

This could be used to give our NHS workers a pay rise?

I would abolish the House of Lords immediately and save what would be a great deal of pay day allowances and travel expenses!

The House of Lords is simply *not* a smart investment.

# TV LICENSE

One word:

*Abolish.*

Like the House of Lords, this system is outdated, overly expensive with very little value.

To compare this to other services, Netflix standard membership is £10.99, Disney's £9.99, Prime £8.99. TV License, for the BBC, Channel 4 and 5 - £13.79.

Not only has the standard of television from these channels dropped to its lowest point, it is the most expensive.

I mean, the BBC pay Gary Lineker to work 2 hours every weekend £1.35 *million* pounds. That's round about £26,000 an episode, £13,000 an hour. I mean *really*?

Maybe drop the astronomical wages and reduce the fee?

Or invest in decent content, like the Premier League? Bundesliga? House of Dragons? Just something worthwhile watching.

It is not value for money, I would abolish the TV License or Tax and end the royal charter with the BBC.

Abolish! Next!

# HOUSING

housing is an issue exacerbated by uncontrolled immigration. With immigration controls in place, this will gradually tip the scales to more people leaving the UK than arriving. This will reduce the demand for Housing and help us maintain our green belts.

**Commit to building zero new build homes in the next 3 years.**

**Start a scheme to repurpose existing buildings and building sites to create new housing.**

**Introduce a rental price cap of maximum 35% uplift of the monthly mortgage value of the accommodation, to be charged per calendar month to keep renting sustainable.**

**Make Tenant Liability Insurance Mandatory.**

**Extend the Equity Loan Scheme to cover existing(old) builds.**

**Propose the introduction of the zero deposit mortgage scheme.**

Having only recently managed to myself get on the property ladder, I very much know the struggle required to achieve this. I very reluctantly had to move into my mother in laws, with my wife and kids.

I had spent the previous 5 years, renting with my partner, paying around £1000 a month for the privilege.

I then found myself having to find a deposit of £10,000 to buy a house. Which being on an average salary and paying £1000 a month in rent and *then* bills, is impossible to do. We came to the gloomy conclusion we would have to move into our parents' house to achieve this. We were lucky in the sense we had parents with a big enough house to accommodate this, but for a newly wed couple this was not easy.

I asked myself then, why do I have to save up for a deposit this big, when we have proven we can pay it, as we have being paying more in rent anyway?

This is the situation countless people and families find themselves in, and it is simply unfair.

After two and a half years of saving, we were ready. We found we were able to do this by using the governments equity loan scheme. The only problem with this, was that it was only applicable to new build houses. Me and my wife were never fans of new builds and much preferred older builds, they are generally cheaper, bigger and better built!

This again made no sense to me, why cut out a vast majority of potential housing? It must only be due to profit reasons, I suppose the value of a new build will only go up. But it is not sustainable. This is why I would change the scheme to include existing builds.

We cannot continue to pop up new houses and expect the same standard of living.

We should move away from this continual drain of our resources and environment and look at more sustainable approaches.

As discussed before, this will be more achievable, when immigration is under control, and the numbers coming in are reducing.

But I would take a bold approach, and commit to building NO new houses for the next 3 years (no new build housing sites).

Let's instead look at repurposing what we have, what lays abandoned and derelict. Land that is already built on, but not used. Not green land and green belts, but wasted grey land! Let's renovate our concrete jungles to be more practical and provide housing. Let's think more sustainable.

We also need to maintain as best we can, availability and affordability, we can do this by introducing the 0% deposit mortgages, with this

being possible by the government acting as a guarantor for the first 5 years, for a small fee. This will provide peace of mind to the mortgage lenders and create more availability.

For those that cannot afford to buy, or indeed do not want to buy, we have seen an unimaginable increase to rental fees. We need to impose a cap on these fees, this should be in the region of a maximum 35% uplift of the monthly mortgage value of the accommodation, spread across the calendar year.

But also, there needs to be more security for the landlords, I believe it should be mandatory for all tenants to have Tenant Liability Insurance to provide this security.

# TRANSPORT

Transport in the UK is probably the worst in Europe. This has been getting gradually more ineffective and expensive as we go on, this is what I would do to remedy this:

**Create a 5 year plan to create a collaborative private and state run transport service, with this in place, we can create the following:**

**Cheaper fares.**

**Penalties for late services or service disruption to provide a more efficient service.**

I would then apply the following:

**Increase the train lines, renovating disused lines and rebuilding derelict stations.**

**In central cities, look to build tramline systems to reduce the flow of traffic.**

**Increase transport services to rural areas.**

It constantly astounds me how poor our public transport system is in the UK. We are continuously plagued by delays, price hikes and inconsistency.

This is highlighted more when you go abroad and experience different countries in Europe's transport systems.

I recently went on a trip with my brother and father to Italy. I was instantly amazed at how cheap and efficient these services were. For example, we flew to Pisa and got the train from Pisa to Florence, this trip took around 1 hour and 20 minutes, and cost a total of £14. Here if I was to go to Bristol Temple Meads from Exeter St Davids, this would take 1 hour and 20 minutes, and cost £33. Why? And you can sure, that journey would be plagued by delays and the dreaded 'Replacement bus services'.

How are we this inefficient? Another example, I went to Majorca and took the bus journey to a nearby beach, this was a 40 minute journey. It cost me €4. Here I took what was meant to be a 25 minute bus journey to the local town centre. The first bus didn't turn up, when the next bus eventually turned up – late – I was then charged £6 for the pleasure. There were delays arriving, so in total with my bus journey back, in which two buses didn't turn up. It took five hours. Five hours in what should of been a 50 minute journey. How?

What can be a downside to privatising a service, is lack of accountability.

I do not believe we are currently in state to nationalise the transport services, but we should be collaborating with them to maintain consistency. We should adopt a format of a part state, part privatised service. Here penalties should be given for poor service and availability.

We should also aim to reduce fares for all services to a more realistic level.

How can we expect more people to use public transport when it is ineffective and we are pricing people out of it.

If we need examples, they are all around us. Why don't look at what our European neighbours are doing and emulate this. They are doing this on a larger scale and more effectively.

In terms of availability, our land is littered with derelict unused train tracks and networks.

Let's start an initiative to renovate and restore these lines and increase availability. This would surely boost the economy and jobs, though would probably be unpopular in our current government because it is not London centric.

We need to look at alternative transport methods in main cities to reduce the traffic congestion and promote cleaner air. These are obvious solutions but required thinking outside of the box.

Where we cannot provide train services, we need to be providing more bus services.

There are still places in rural areas where buses do not run on Sundays or services run from 9am to 2pm.

In this day and age this should be a thing of the past.

We are just so ridiculously poor at this, that someone needs to make a change. It is not even a main focus in any manifesto I have seen from the Labour Party or Conservatives.
Come on political parties! Get your act together.

# COMMUNITES

To increase community facilities and support. I would do the following:

**Increase funding for community projects, such as litter picking, wild gardening.**

**Increase Youth Centres with skill based workshops.**

**Provide support for an increase in the Neighbourhood Watch scheme.**

**Increase the amount you can claim back under Gift Aid to 25%.**

There is currently a disconnect in our communities. This was further exacerbated by the covid pandemic and divisive politics. Also hindered by the society of the keyboard warriors of the social media world.

There is almost a rhetoric of 'do not trust thy neighbour'.

The togetherness that was in abundance during the immediate post war era is gone. This is a result of the times we are living in and the lack of investment in society. The focus of togetherness has been replaced with the drive of expansion.

Small towns are now almost extinct, now we have to find new ways to bring about a community feel, with a community that is triple the size.

This is no easy task, believe it or not, one of the few things that tends to bring people together is big national events, the Royal family are the advocates of this. The events they hold always pull together a community of thousands to celebrate or watch in awe of the splendour. None did this better than our late Queen Elizabeth II.

But what do we do outside of this, to level up communities and create the 'spirit'? I would start with increasing community events and projects.

When I was young, I grew up in the outskirts of a large city, here we had an annual festival, the community would get together and run stalls and entertainment and 'Tug of War' tournaments.

For one day, this brought everyone together and we all thrived, businesses made significant profits. Partnerships and friendships were formed.

Where I grew up has since expanded, the council that looked after it has changed and looks after a larger area. The festival no longer exists.

We need to bring these events back to boost our communities.

We need to run projects that benefit the community, litter picking sessions, fund raisers for local projects, like skate parks for kids or the construction of a community pool. These things bring people closer, working towards a common goal that benefits all.

We need to invest in our youth, and increase youth centre availability, but properly organised and run ones!

When I was young we use to have a youth centre, it just played music and you could go there to hang out and get up to everything you shouldn't.

If this is run properly, you could run workshops. Workshops on learning different skill sets, like carpentry, cooking or to learn what investing is all about, money management for the future. This is just a few things we could teach.

If invest in our youth we will get so much more out of them. A school cannot teach everything, but everything should be available to learn, we do not invest enough in this country in life skills which our European counterparts do.
I believe we also need to increase participants in the old institution of the Neighbourhood Watch. These people help monitor and deter anti-social and criminal behaviour in towns and cities. An extra pair of eyes to help the local authorities and it also boosts the community feel, when you are looking after where you live. As the community spirit has slowed ebbed this

organisation has waned, it would be a loss to our communities to see it become a thing of the past.

Now, one pivotal part of a community are it's businesses, they bring in jobs, economic growth and enrichment. A sign of a good business is one that looks to give back to the community it trades in. We see many business do this, this ranges from giving to local charities, to sponsoring local football teams.

These businesses are assets to the local community and we need to attract more local businesses to follow suit, so I would propose an increase to Gift Aid by 5%.

With these proposals, as well as more police on the streets, a better, fairer welfare and housing system, and an improved transport system, should bring about stronger, more together communities that we would all want to be a part of.

# FARMING

## AND

# FISHERIES

We are finding more and more that the food farmed in this country is sent abroad, I believe this now requires change, this is how I would do this:

**Provide farmers with grants when produce is sold in the UK, to UK resident retailers.**

**Increase the grants provided to UK Farmers for when green and sustainable methods are used.**

**Reduce and streamline regulations to improve and make more efficient processes by recommendation of Farming industry experts.**

**Maintain the funding for the UK Seafood Fund.**

**Increase the UK Farming fund in line with inflation.**

**Provide military support where required to create a secure environment for our fisherman and to protect our fishing waters.**

Let me make something clear first. I am by no means, any kind of expert in the way of Farming. These issues I raise may not be the pivotal ones, but these are the issues that are brought more to my attention from an outsiders perspective. So Farmers and Fishermen, please forgive me if I completely miss the point! But just know, I was not educated at Eton, just a standard secondary school, in a city, no where near a farm. So again, my apologies.

One thing that stands out to me, is when you walk around your local Tesco, or most of the other big supermarket brands, is less and less of what we grow in the UK, is *actually* sold in the UK.

This now stands at just 60% of food grown in the UK, to be sold in the UK.

This to me, is also partially driven by the love of the fruits and meats produced here becoming less and less. When was the last time anyone bought some gooseberries? I know if I asked my children, they probably wouldn't know what they are! Other produce like Rhubarb is becoming less popular.

We also do not take enough advantage of our local game - deer, pheasant and rabbit. Many farmers would tell you they actually lose a considerable amount in vegetation damage from browsing deer. Why do we not utilise the meat of venison more? Make this a more common place meat to use. It seems we could do with bringing out our nan's old cooking books and making use of them!

One subject that is of concern, is the environmental impact farming is having in the UK.

The impact of the expansion of farmland, has had a massive detrimental effect to our natural world, not just in the UK, but around the world. A staggering 44% of habitable land in the world is now used for agriculture.

Not only has the vast surge of farmland had an impact, but the processes used on this land, is not only killing the local wildlife, but actually damaging the soil in which we grow the food.

We need to change these processes, the beauty of it, is most of the damage is reversible. But it won't always be.

The sooner we research new practices and embrace existing greener ones, the quicker we can reverse this.

We need to increase our wildland and start to actively look after our natural world and starting more sustainable farming practices will help towards this.

In terms of Fisheries, the environmental processes also need to be increased, more protected 'no fishing' waters are needed to increase fish counts.

Introduce more criteria for trawlers to fish sustainably, to stop what is a devastating impact to marine life.

We have also seen more disputes between our different nations fishermen, on where to fish. So I would ensure if this continues, that royal naval vessels are deployed to protect UK fishing territory.

# BUSINESS

# &

# TRADE

With the High Street becoming more and more derelict, how can we attract more business to our High Street?

This is what I would do:

**With the previous suggested renting cap, this will attract more small businesses.**

**The reduction in Corporation Tax will attract bigger businesses.**

**Maintain current business loans offered by the current government.**

**Provide guidance to councils to effectively use funding to renovate town centres.**

**Continue Renegotiations with EU for a better trade deal.**

**Make a direct effort to complete further trade deals with Non-EU countries.**

**Make income protection insurance for Sole Traders mandatory.**

We have seen our economy take a hit over recent years, due to unforeseen global events, including the war in Ukraine and Covid.

There were unwise policies introduced during covid by our now prime minister Rishi Sunak (though it is July 4th 2024 whilst I am writing this, so tomorrow, there may very well be a new one!).

These included the grants that were introduced for Sole Traders.

Though helpful, the policy details that was created for them, seemed to be so rushed and fragmented, that there were so many loopholes, it was left open to abuse. My god did people abuse them!

I have several friends who are sole trader builders and these people continued (rightfully or wrongfully) to trade during the pandemic. In fact, their businesses boomed! As everyone was stuck inside, it was then people decided to renovate.

These friends were laughing, as they we getting paid and claiming £15,000 in grants on top of this.

It was a rushed, not thought through policy, which cost the tax payer billions.

£7.6 billion to be precise.

These payments should *never* of been grants. They should have been trackable, low to 0% interest loans.

Off the back of this, I would of thought we would of learnt and made income protection insurance mandatory for a sole traders, to stop this happening again.

The damage done by this one act, was immeasurable. Well, I suppose actually, it is measurable, it was £7.6 billion worth of damage.

This on review for me, is a sackable offence. But he is our Prime Minister (*currently*) instead.

In terms of the high street, the way we shop has changed, with more and more people choosing to shop online, this is naturally going to put a strain on the high street.

With that in mind, we need to look at what struggles the high shops face, to see if we can reduce them.

I know in my local area, one thing that really adds strain and deters businesses from starting up in the area, is rental fees. These fees in this particular area of Devon are astronomical. Especially when you can go 20 mins up the road and they are greatly reduced. Funnily enough, that high street is booming with all the latest trendy and up market brands.

Applying the rental caps I propose would help to resolve this issue and help the high street recover. A better transport system, will resolve the convenience issue.

We need to attract the bigger foreign corporations to invest in the United Kingdom, a reduction to the increased current corporation tax rate will do this.

We can help do this, by closing loop holes in the law that allows certain big businesses to pay less tax or avoid it altogether.
We need to advise our councils more on how to start renovating our high street. This has already happened to our large cities in the UK. This now needs to start happening in the smaller towns.

The money provided in some instances, is just not being spent wisely.

We then have Brexit. This was a golden opportunity to boost current business deals and create new and more exciting ones. This rhetoric that no one wants to do business with the UK, so we were better off in the EU, is absolute rubbish.

We did business deals before we were in it, there is no reason we shouldn't be able to after.

What happened is we had either incompetent leaders or an incompetent and inefficient parliament.

Because the vote on Brexit was close, closer than expected, there was division. It was everywhere, in households, in businesses and in parliament. The people that voted to remain, refused to accept the outcome of a democratic vote.

They were wrong.

What happened next, was instead of accepting this, there were rebellions. Left, right and centre, the remainers were stopping proposed bills and stopping the legislation going through to make Brexit happen.

We became a laughing stock on the international stage, our bargaining chips were made meaningless, by the selfish few who did not like it when democracy didn't work for them.

This made making decent trade deals near impossible. Now we are a few years past and most MP's have now accepted the result, it is the time to go back to the negotiating table.

We need to first work on trade deals outside of the EU, strengthen and make new deals. Once this is achieved, we then need to go back to the negotiating table with the European Union, in what should be a better position of power.

The EU needs an increase in profit, just as the UK does and as we are the world's 6th largest economy, they will want to trade with us.

But if the person you are trading with is in turmoil, you know you are in a position of power in that trade.

This can be easily remedied and should be, as better trade relationships with our European neighbours will benefit us all

.

# CLIMATE

# &

# THE
# ENVIRONMENT

---

Climate change is a very real threat the will fundamentally change our way of life. We need to take action now to affect the future.

This is what I propose to help with that:

**Manufacturing of Petrol and Diesel vehicles to be stopped by 2030.**

**With the idea to phase out Petrol and Diesel vehicle use by 2040.**

**This will be supported by the reconfiguring and improvement of our public transport offerings.**

**Create a Global Climate collaborative committee to share renewable energy technology between the worlds countries and firms.**

**UK target of 90% of farming and fishing processes to be sustainable and environmentally friendly by 2030.**

**Increase natural wild land by 10% by 2030.**

**Create nature Highways where possible through busy road networks.**

**The halting of new build houses to protect green belts.**

Increase conservation projects for endangered and threatened species.

Increase border controls to reduce the risk of invasive species.

Look at ways to protect local wildlife by implementing relevant culls or hunts to reduce badger and deer numbers where needed.

Promote the consumption of game to better maintain numbers, whilst boosting economic growth.

Begin a grow your own project to promote self-sustainability and increase wildlife friendly environments.

Ban single use plastic in all retail sectors by 2030.

We all know the challenges we face going forward with our climate. There can no longer be any suggestion that climate change is not real or is 'scaremongering'.

It is very much here and we are starting to feel the effects. More so third world countries, which perhaps is why the urgency for the western world to act has lagged so much.

We *have* to come to terms with the fact, that the way of life as we know it, now cannot continue, it is not sustainable and we are at that point where this will become more real.

It is time to pick people over profit.

Now there is most certainly profit to be made from renewable energy and new technology to help create more sustainable methods. So businessmen should not fear a drop in fortune, but they now need to change their focus to new ventures.

We need to stick to what was originally announced and stop production of petrol and diesel vehicles by 2030. We cannot delay this, the effect this would bring was demonstrated by the recent event of the covid pandemic.

When lock down was imposed, the streets and highways emptied, all major cities were brought to a standstill.

What happened in the days following this, was a complete change in our weather system, in our environment. The world started to recover.

We had cleaner air and better weather, this shows the impact that the millions of cars pumping out fumes every hour of the day has on the environment.

By doing this and sticking to it, the car industry has time to adjust and invest adequately.

This should lead to all petrol and diesel vehicles being phased out by 2040.

With an improved public transport system in place this will make the transition easier.

In many of the other polices I have suggested, we have hit environmental suggestions within them, including the change to most farming and fishing processes to become sustainable.

The increase of wild land, to help rejuvenate the UK's natural world.

We need to look at what countries around the world are doing to help better the environment, like formation of 'nature highways' in busy road networks. These are essentially tunnels created below busy roads, to allow wildlife to migrate across these busy roads safely.

We need to create more green spaces or conservation areas to help protect our wildlife and especially our bird species.

What will be crucial in tackling climate change and becoming sustainable, is collaboration. We can't alone, make a big enough impact to make a change. But we can spear head it and become the trend setter.

We need to collaborate with all nations, sharing technology and ideas and knowledge on sustainable processes.

This does not mean we have to spend billions to do this, we only need to meet and talk. If resources are provided, this can be an exchange of resources, all with one global purpose. To preserve the world for our children and their children.

This is the way forward.

How we get there as a nation, we have touched upon already.

Reduce building new houses, renovate and innovate instead.

Review our most or near endangered species and as a government, introduce conservation plans. Not just to stick them in a zoo, but to reintroduce them into the wild. We have seen success stories with this already with otters and beavers being successfully reintroduced in the UK.

But like the story of the UK's red squirrel, we also need to have tougher, more thorough checks on imported goods, to stop the spread of invasive species.

As mentioned in the farming section, we need to promote the consumption of game, this will help keep deer numbers in check and add additional UK produce to the shelves.

There was brief push in prior years to promote self-sustainability by growing your own vegetables. This needs a further push, especially among schools to help teach horticulture to the next generation. With even the potential to reduce food costs for schools.

One major change, which we have the opportunity to spear head is the ban of single use plastics, in every retail sector. This should only be needed for medical purposes only.

This is not as difficult to achieve as many will have you believe and many food producers are already converting to this.

We need to collaborate with our global partners to come up with a method to remove all plastic from our oceans.

I mean, I suppose we couldn't just gather it all up and send it on rocket into the sun? or Jupiter? Just a thought!

# SCOTLAND

In terms of Scotland, we had the Scottish independence referendum in 2014, at which the overall decision was to remain.

I believe it should always be Scotland's right to decide to hold a referendum on independence, as it should be for Wales and Northern Ireland also.

The terms of that separation however, should *always* remain the same. They would not and *should* not be able to continue using the pound. They would need start their own currency.

Funding that is currently provided for University fees and other such benefits would cease.

The nations nuclear deterrent would need to be moved to UK territory.

Independence would mean, independence.

These issues alone, were why the majority of the population of Scotland decided 'No' for independence.

But the option for it, should *never* be taken away, as that is every countries                       basic                       rights.

# Conclusion

So this is what I believe should be in place for future.

I am not a privately schooled child, what I have learnt about politics, I have learnt myself, or from my father, so please forgive me if some of these policies are unpolished.

I have covered what I believe should be the main focuses for any government that comes to power. Common sense issues, climate, taxes, immigration, and education.

The point that is one of the most important, is to start to give the nation the tools needed to make educated decisions. Not having to be completely reliant on the information provided by media outlets, which can be manipulated and corrupt. This is where we are now, people are disillusioned with politics, because they do not know enough about it. With this knowledge, we as a people would not accept governments that do not act in our interests and are ineffective.

Everyone can see the climate change impact, but we have no government that will take action on it. Immigration that seems to have no limits.

This is why people are disillusioned.

We need to make a change, and with the knowledge to do this we can command a stronger nation that demands more action to tackle the vital issues.

I admit I have not done the costings for my policies, but have where best possible, tried to include savings, where I have entered costs.

I hope it at least offers an opinion which is not manipulated and tarnished by the pursuit of political power and wealth.

In any case, if not, this book should be a good size to prop up a wobbly table, thank you for reading!


Yours Always,


J.K. Adams.

Printed in Great Britain
by Amazon

45208062R00059